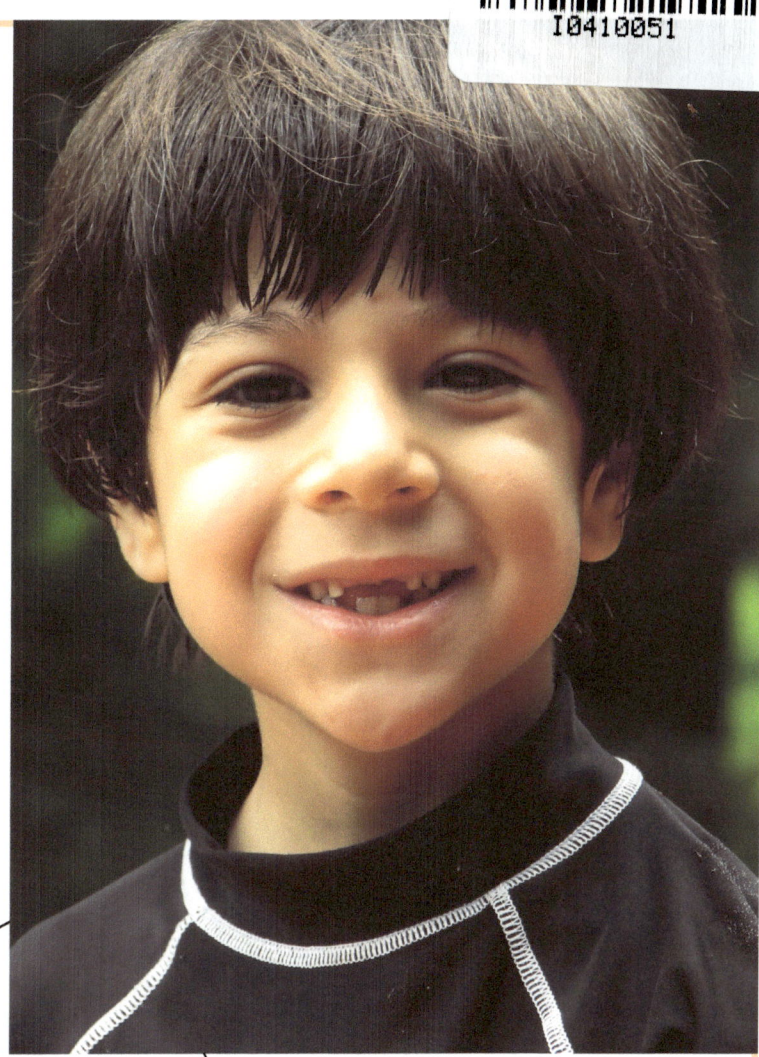

Adventures In Autism

PEDRO GOES TO SCHOOL

Written by Amy Arnold

Pedro Goes to School
Adventures in Autism Series
Amy M. Arnold, M.S.Ed.

Copyright © 2011 by Amy M. Arnold:
First Edition, 2011
ISBN-13: 978-1466458659

ISBN-10: 1466458658

Photography courtesy of FreeStockPhotos.Biz.

http://www.freestockphotos.biz/stockphoto/5410

For my family...
My beautiful daughters, Lauren and Emily
My loving husband, Stephen
My mom, Rachel
My brother, Michael
And my nephew, Jacob

They taught me that family means love!

Meet Pedro! He is going to be a student in your class this year. Pedro is very much like you, and he is also very different from you. We are all different, and everyone is differently-abled!

Pedro likes to play on the playground. His favorite thing to do is to hang from the monkey bars. Sometimes he will forget to ask you to play with him. You could ask him to play with you! Don't be afraid to ask when you want to play with someone.

Pedro has autism. This means he might have a hard time telling you what he needs or how he feels. Sometimes he does not understand what the teacher or his friends want him to do.

Do you ever misunderstand or wonder what the teacher wants you to do? It can be a scary feeling!

But if you remember that we all get confused sometimes, you will know how to help your friend, Pedro.
You can talk softly to him and help him to understand. Be patient with your friends, and they will be patient with you!

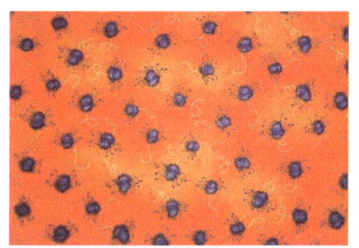

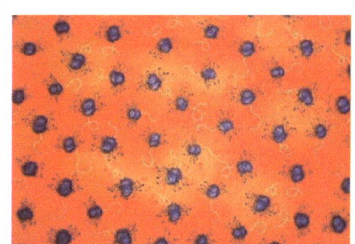

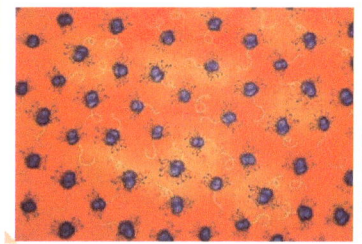

Pedro has a big family. He has one sister and three brothers. His family likes to do things together.

Sometimes his brothers tease him and make him feel very sad. Do you have brothers or sisters that tease you? If you do, then you can understand how Pedro feels.

But sometimes, his brothers and sister play games like Capture the Flag. They will play and climb at the playground. This makes Pedro happy, and he feels loved.
Pedro smiles a lot when he feels like an important part of his family.

Pedro sometimes gets upset or angry. You might not understand why. Your teacher may not understand why. Pedro might not even understand why!

When someone has autism, they can get very angry or scared, and we may not know why. What should we do?

When Pedro gets angry, you can just sit with him and be very still and quiet. That will let him know that someone cares. It might also help him to calm down.

After you feel angry, sometimes you feel very tired. If Pedro does not want to talk, please remember that he is still your friend!

But sometimes, we need to focus on the teacher because she can help Pedro to settle down and be calm again.

The teacher might need to think about the best way to help Pedro. She will need the class to stay on task so she can help Pedro or another child in the class.

Many children will need help in different ways. You will need help from the teacher, too!

The teacher's job is to help all the students, and she is happy to do it!

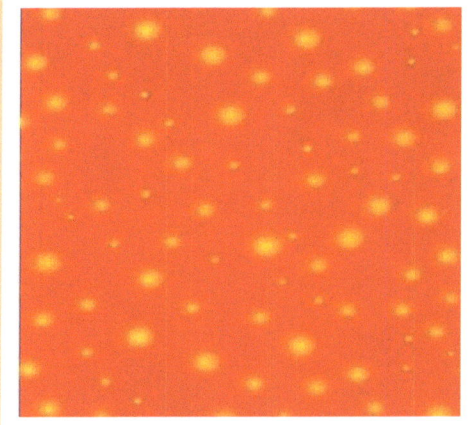

Everything does not always go the way we expect, but as long as we work together, everyone will learn and grow!

Even though Pedro has autism, he is still a student just like you!
He likes to drink from the water fountain. He likes to play on the playground. He likes to have friends and feel loved.

Pedro may need more help with his school work. Many students need extra help with school work. Pedro may not read as well as you, but he may love doing math!

Pedro will have good days and bad days, just like you! That's why we all have to work together as friends.

Pedro wants to be your friend, but he might not know the right words to say to get you to play with him. Being a good listener and a kind person will help Pedro to feel more comfortable with you.

Sometimes he might not understand your body language. That is what you do with your hands and face. You can make someone feel unsafe or make them feel like you are a friend, depending on your body language. Be sure you are always kind so no one will think you are a bully!

We can all make loud noises when we are being silly. Sometimes Pedro will make loud noises, and you might not understand why.

Please don't make loud noises in return. Pedro will not be able to calm down if the classroom is full of other loud noises.

If you were upset or scared, you would want others to be calm and considerate of your feelings. So try to focus on your teacher and stay on task. Then she will be able to help Pedro.

Pedro might run away from the group. That doesn't mean that he doesn't like you. It doesn't mean he doesn't like his teacher.

Sometimes when we get angry, we run away because we don't know what else to do. Remember that when Pedro comes back to the group, he will need a kind friend!

Pedro is a lot like you. He loves to play, he wants to have friends, and he wants to be happy.

He does his school work, and he climbs on the jungle gym. He has good days and bad days, just like you!

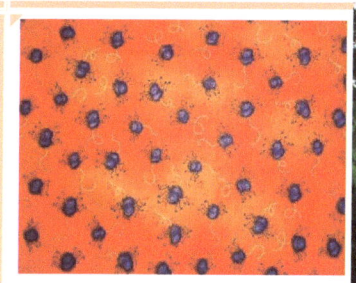

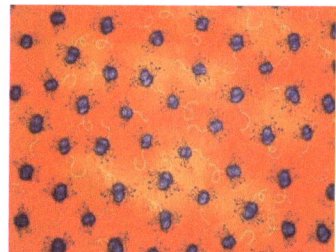

Even though Pedro has autism, he still
wants to talk and share with his friends.
He may not always know the right words.
He may not always know just how to let you
know that he wants to be your friend.
But he does!

Will you be
Pedro's friend?

I hope so!

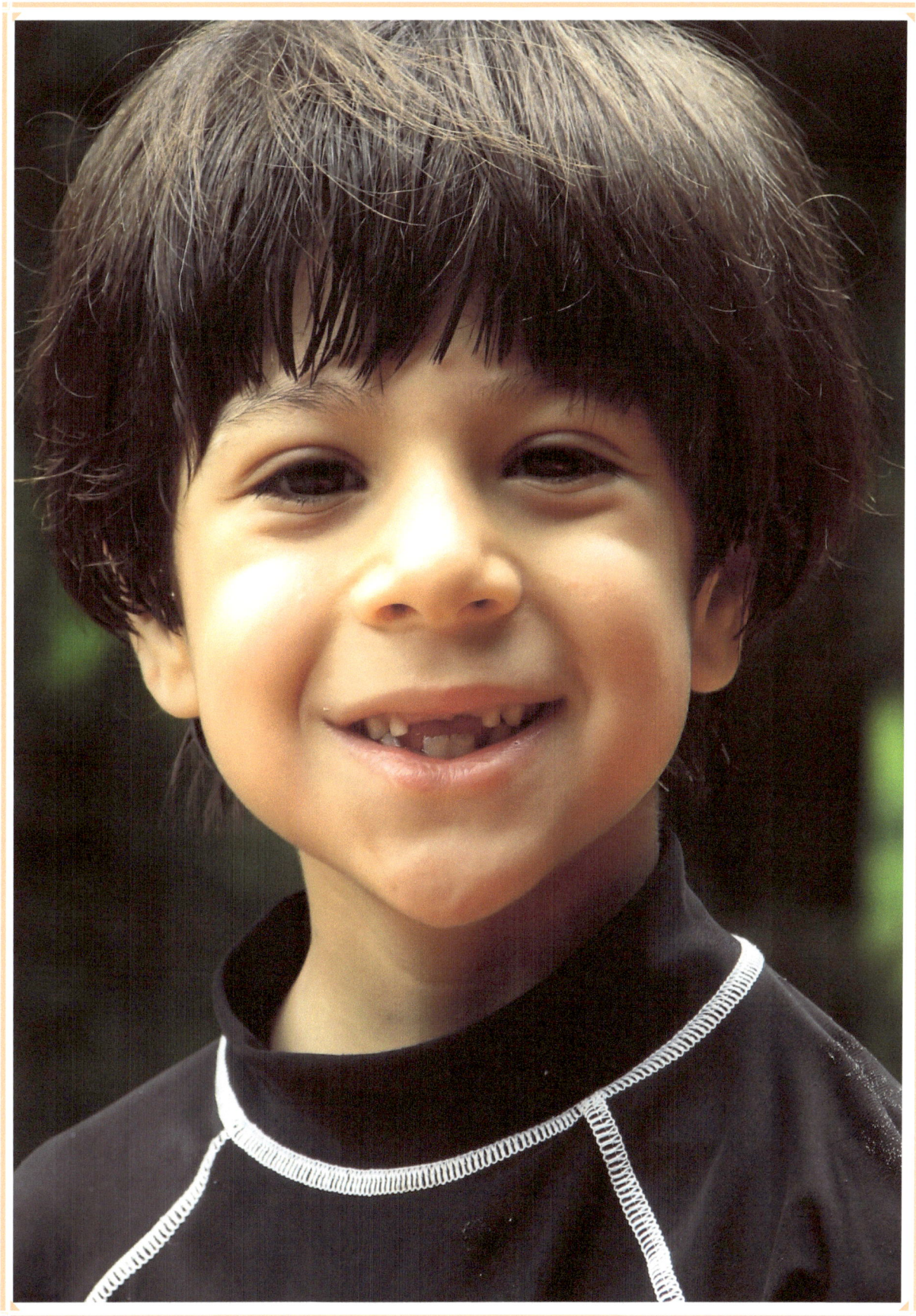

Adventures in Autism Series

What is autism?

Autism is a condition that affects the ability to communi-cate, to control emotions and responses, and to accept change.

Who has autism?
Many people of all ages can have autism. One in 110 people have autism.

Where do people live that have autism?
People with autism live everywhere!

How can I help someone with autism?
Be yourself and treat them like a friend!